random
reflections

Mental Multi-Vitamins

Des O'Donnell

Published by Messenger Publications, 2022

ISBN: 9781788125864

Designed by Messenger Publications Design Department
Cover background image © Shutterstock
Typeset in Times New Roman and URW Din condensed
Printed by Hussar Books

Messenger Publications,
37 Leeson Place, Dublin D02 E5V0, Ireland
www.messenger.ie

introduction

introduction

With the passing years, one of my major learnings has been that to live a full life in the modern world, it is necessary to grow into conscious critical awareness of what one is experiencing. The speed of modern life makes it necessary to pause often and to reflect. Otherwise, life flows over us and away from us; we live with surface feelings and emotions without deep thought or consciousness.

Throughout my later years, I have developed the practice of writing down my thoughts and some phrases that nourished my mind. This little booklet contains 700 of these that I consider creative.

I offer them to the reader, not to amuse or to entertain, but as invitations to think, to reflect or to learn and maybe to be fruitfully confused. The full meaning of each one may not be immediately obvious. In fact, some of them could disturb the person willing to be stretched in their beliefs, in their style of thinking and perhaps in their behaviour.

To gain most from the exercise of going through them, it is best to ponder them one at a time and to resist skimming from one to the next. It would be best to pause after reading one and to think about its meaning.

If it encourages you, grasp it.

If it disturbs you, ask yourself why.

If it amuses you, pause to enjoy it.

If it puzzles you, work on it.

This booklet can be kept in your pocket or handbag to offer you a nugget to reflect on when you are free.

Some will find it helpful to go through it with a friend or in a discussion group.

- It is becoming clearer that we now live in a world of common fate and responsibility.

- Modern life has to be increasingly lived with less experience of distance in time and space.

- Over the past 60 years, we have moved from a culture of authority into a culture of choice.

- To prevent conversation or dialogue can be a subtle form of violence.

- We do not own a single day because we cannot store it or ever get it back.

- Carl Jung reminds us that life flows from springs that are both clear and muddy.

- In a time of hype and fake news, the first things I must always communicate are credibility and caring.

- Comfort and luxury will not make us happy. Someone to love and something to be enthusiastic about will.

- Always listen beyond the words, for the other's feelings, frame of reference and for their intention if possible.

- Our parents did not give the world to us; it was loaned to us by our children.

- A voyage of discovery is not seeking new places. It is developing new eyes and a spirit of curiosity.

- In a time of change, learners learn, but the learned can remain equipped for a world that is gone.

- Many people live with the absence of presence. They lack simple self-awareness.

- Life today is marked by proximity and exchange rather than by distance and deference.

- Truth and authenticity can be refreshing in an age of hype and spin.

- Faced with so much change today, we need discernment and decision, not defence and denial.

- Life today may be more about participating in a process than finding answers.

- Media 'news' today is often shallow, slanted, repetitive, opinionative and untruthful.

- The modern person has heightened expectations but difficulty with long commitment.

- If you wish to prevent change, avoid reading or meeting new people.

- The provision of comfortable convenience can easily lead to cosy complacency.

- Modern life helps us to limit prolonged procrastination.

- Diversity is divine. Division is diabolical.

- We are moving from the experience of authority – rigid and flexible – to the authority of experience – good and bad.

- Isolating individualism and captivating consumerism are growing today.

- Today we need depth to face relativity, patience with contingency and security before impermanency.

- In today's plentifulness I must live an active asceticism that often says 'enough'.

- Asking if it is causality, coincidence, providence or chance is difficult today.

- Today we must increase global connectivity and deepen global consciousness.

- Deep choice and prolonged commitment are culturally unsupported today.

- The Church must now try to be yeast, as it becomes less a city on the hill in the modern world.

- Modern life can call Christians to be more searchers than believers.

- The loudness of have-to-do-ness in modern life wrecks the joy of hearing your own music.

- There seem to be less centres and fewer margins in modern life.

- In the modern world feelings are increasingly beginning to matter more than facts.

- Modern people need to see different signs of God's presence than did people did in the past.

- In free countries what was a culture of accepted authority is becoming a culture of choice.

- Identity becomes a big question in changing, divided or polarised communities.

- Be alert to the tyranny of the 'urgent' and the oppression of the 'must have'.

- Excess money is not the problem. It's the acquisitive urge for 'moreness'.

- With the disappearance of metanarratives, subjective interpretations tend to thrive.

- Churches must move from domination to dialogue, from conquest to conversation.

- Not by phones alone doth man or woman live.

- Let us try to reveal to one another the amazement of being human.

- Be aware of the emptiness of affluence and the perversity of advertising.

- Criticism is never limited by lack of knowledge.

- The new experience of the present always needs the tested memory of the past.

- Bureaucracy can bury common decency.

- Scientific progress sometimes grows faster than wisdom in the human mind.

- In this age of fake news, we all need to become fact-finders, proofreaders and critical editors.

- Protest in large numbers. Learn in small groups.

- Excess can be a substitute for genuine enjoyment.

- Talking nonsense can be pardonable provided that it is not done solemnly or in a loud voice.

- Screens can deliver messages. Only humans can convey meaning.

- We are now living with the disappearance of distance and with telescoped time.

- Are we moving towards a totally anthropocentric culture run by a team of technocrats?

- Disorder is not final disaster. Planet earth came from a collapsing cloud of dust.

- Signs can only point. Symbols can influence and stimulate.

- Is my wisdom keeping up with my participation in the unparalleled scientific progress of our time?

- Technology has moved from being facilitative, to being transformative to being almost creative.

- The economy of consumerism is colonizing the human heart.

- Constant stimulation is no substitute for reflective moments or for in-depth conversation.

- A culture of superficiality, provisionality, individualism and instancy seems to be emerging.

- A majority can mean that all the self-interested people are on the same side.

- Which of my old certainties are evaporating? It may help to put them on paper.

- Grab-and-go meals are injurious to our minds and our bodies.

- Some people will believe anything if it is whispered to them.

- History records only one indispensable man – Adam.

- We live in a time of increased communication but maybe of less communion.

- The four speeds of prayer are slow, slower, pause and reverse.

- Without introduction and commentary, the Bible is a dangerous book.

- Good preaching is naming and encouraging goodness in the human experience.

- Religion and rules can wrap and bind. Faith and relationships release us and set us free.

- Pope Francis tells us that the Church is a hospital for sinners, not a rest home for saints.

- Sin is less breaking a law than blurring God's image in me.

- Faith can be helped by temples, mosques and churches, by doctrines or dogmas, but these do not create it.

- Kind deeds are a fruit of grace, not a source of grace.

- As a believer, the authentic needs of others are sources of my salvation.

- Exclusive male leadership can defeminize and damage the human.

- Sometimes the only response to prayer is the grace to keep on praying.

- St Paul reminds us that we are all prophets when we build up, encourage and reassure.

- Could there be more faith in honest doubt than in half our creeds?

- False religion imposes and makes demands. Authentic religion invites and bestows.

- Faith might have more to do with the cosmos we inhabit than with the church we attend.

- Mary was a poor peasant whose son disturbed the system. She was present at his execution.

- God promises believers a safe landing but not a smooth passage.

- Jesus does not call just believers. He calls disciples who will follow him through suffering love to the cross.

- Contemplation takes place when I am reflectively and compassionately aware.

- When the hand ceases to scatter the heart ceases to pray.

- With spirituality, it is not a hard grinding effort that counts; it is gracious, loving surrender.

- The sacred is to be found in the ordinary, in one's own backyard.

- Every organisation – even Churches – must wear the hair shirt of its history.

- Materialism, moralism, measuring and magic are enemies of faith.

- The Church sometimes asks us to squeeze our experience into a doctrine when it does not fit our present development.

- Simone Weil reminds us that Christianity is not a separate religion; it's a healing message for all religions.

- Prayer is more about trust and hope than about arranging the world to suit me.

- Our parish church is a building we worship in. The cosmos is a church we live in.

- For most people, holy stories are not evidence. Searchers need to see the Gospel in the present tense.

- Faith cannot be passed on. Only the disposition to receive it can be encouraged.

- People will die for their faith. Others will kill for their religion.

- Spirituality is not conceptual, organisational or doctrinal; it is relational.

- Unbelieving critics and uncritical believers seem unable to walk quietly on the journey of faith.

- Dogma and discipline are boundaries not sources.

- The Incarnation is happening as I become more human.

- Science is a search for explanations. Faith is a search for meaning.

- Faith includes trusting in advance what will make sense only later.

- Faith and doubt are more verbs than nouns. We are all faith-ing and doubting.

- Faith is not the pursuit of perfection. It is patient growth in trusting love.

- Measured against the existence of the cosmos, Christianity is just two seconds old.

- Liturgy is not stepping out of the secular. It is celebrating the sacred in the secular.

- Faith is trustful commitment, not investigation.

- All false religion can lead to tribalism, exclusivism and to feelings of superiority.

- Is our God too small, our Christ too cosy, our Church too closed and our priesthood too paralysed?

- Some people have only enough religion to keep them uncomfortable.

- Priests should always remember that they are in sales not in management.

- The Kingdom of God is more about goodness, peace and joy than about belief.

- Faith is more about fidelity in action than about fervour of feelings.

- Newman reminds us that real faith does not depend on saintly scenery and sticky sentimentality.

- Faith is sometimes like a tunnel with a dim light at the end of it.

- Christians need not ask for a share in the divine life. They already possess it.

- Sacraments celebrate the grace we live in more than the grace they bring.

- Faith is a personal encounter with the transcendence we call God.

- By faith we share God's love. By the power of his Spirit we mediate it to others.

- Why faith fails to connect with so many good people remains an unanswered question.

- Faith enables us to live peacefully, happily and creatively without having all the answers.

- Real faith is not built on evidence.

- Faith is engagement and trust, not analysis and proof.

- For the person of faith, every bush is burning.

- God's plan is not a future journey. It is a call to growth in faith and love now.

- Religion gives answers. Faith poses questions.

- Fundamentalism is an attempt to move from text to application without explanation.

- A man drowned crossing a stream that averaged four feet deep.

- Has the Church forgotten that people cannot be commanded to celebrate?

- When the Church resorts to the use of power, it fails to trust in the presence of God.

- Since God became flesh, all created things are blessed.

- Many great truths once seemed religiously dangerous.

- Unless my life is permeated by practical compassion, religion does not exist for me.

- Religion may be used as a sedative against popular revolt in unjust political systems.

- An informed compassionate heart must lead to a creation-centred spirituality.

- Spiritual growth cannot be built on imposed religious conformity.

- All activity that is truly human is truly graced.

- I cannot work miracles, but by active loving I can work healing all the time.

- Holiness and healthy wholeness are the same.

- When our hands cease to share, our hearts must cease to pray.

- Sin is putting energy in the wrong channel.

- Some disciplined atheistic doubt can keep us away from false or facile images of God.

- Some believers treat religion as another good to be consumed.

- Science can purify religion from superstition. Religion can purify science from idolatry.

- It is better to pray without parentheses.

- It is fatal to never feel doubtful or hesitant.

- Doubtful apparitions and excessive devotions cannot replace mysticism.

- Religion helps those who fear going to Hell. Spirituality helps those you feel they might be going through it.

- Jesus did not say, 'Where two or three hundred are gathered in my name….'

- Communism is the evidence of the unfulfilled tasks of Christianity.

- The Church is the Eucharist expanded, and the Eucharist is the Church condensed.

- Einstein said that it was by challenging an axiom that he discovered relativity.

- Authentic religion is *ekstasis* (Greek – stepping outside of oneself) much more than believing.

- Inauthentic religion will usually over-depend on empty ritual.

- Religion can be a sedative against creativity in corrupt states and Churches.

- If you allot time to pray and stick to it despite distractions you are praying.

- To believe a doctrine without having had the experience it describes is difficult.

- True contemplation leads to a critical caring awareness of everyone we know and of everything that is.

- Pope John Paul said that the world needs heralds of the Gospel who are experts in humanity.

- Religion is anxious to give answers. Spirituality looks at questions.

- A Church at the centre is privileged. A Church on the margin is where it should be.

- An affair with the Church can destroy your marriage to God.

- Effective prayer is harder on the soles of our shoes than on the seat of our pants.

- Selfishness makes one religiously deaf.

- Scripture can be read fruitfully only for the purpose of personal transformation.

- A good book in your hand is worth two on the shelf.

- Our self-interest always influences our choices and decisions. Where I sit is usually where I stand.

- Prolonged worry is like a photographic darkroom. It develops your negatives.

- Pessimists complain about the wind. Optimists expect it to change. Realists adjust the sails.

- Running one's life on the cafeteria plan of self-service is bad for the friendship business.

- When it is possible today, loving is never for tomorrow.

- Deep laughter can be a brief holiday.

- On your search for pleasure, pause often to let peace catch up with you.

- When you feel that life is difficult, it is good to ask yourself compared with what.

- The antidote to exhaustion is enthusiasm in reflectively doing what we deeply want to do.

- Yes, time flies, but I am the pilot.

- Finding peace of mind sometimes depends on a walk around the lake.

- When you can, live life with energy, enthusiasm and empathy.

- Live so that every morning when you get out of bed, the devil will say 'Damn it; he (or she) is still alive!'

- It is usually easier to keep up than to catch up.

- It is always a mistake to do nothing because I can do just a little.

- I have only now. The past is dead. Tomorrow is hope.

- Ants work hard, but they never miss a picnic.

- Aim at being more rather than having more.

- Happiness comes from faith, enthusiasm, discipline and a little foolishness.

- Intelligence Quotient can get you a job. Emotional Quotient gets you promotion.

- Beware of the high cost of low living.

- Some fragrance always remains on the hand that gives roses.

- If I do not know where you stand, I will fall for anything.

- One kind word can warm up a whole week.

- 'But' can erase all you have said. Better use 'and' or 'although'.

- If time were endless, tomorrow could be used as today's great laboursaving devices.

- The early bird caught the worm, but the early worm was caught.

- Neglecting the present moment is losing all you have.

- How many times did you say 'Thank you' today?

- Worry does not empty tomorrow of its sorrows. It robs today of its strength.

- Don't watch the clock. Do what it is does. Keep going.

- On the voyage of life, disembark for short periods on the islands of stillness.

- Life comes one day at a time so that we can manage it.

- Much of what I will be tomorrow comes from the choices I make today.

- You'll find anything where you put it, not where you left it.

- Before you sleep, name one thing for which you are grateful that day.

- Every new day is another chance to get it right.

- Unless 'I should have' is accompanied by 'but next time', it is useless.

- Update your living environment regularly. It keeps you alert.

- You live only once, but it is enough if you get it right.

- Some things are more than obvious. They are significant.

- Any level of living can be fun. Only deep living can bring joy.

- No matter how you feel, wake up, get up, dress up, show up and try not to give up.

- Turn the light off from time to time and listen to the dark.

- Every truthful personal exchange with another is a growth moment for both.

- We can forget who we are and where we are going unless we stop from time to time.

- People who knows that they speak the truth rarely needs to raise their voice.

- It is not the strongest plant or person that survives. It is the most adaptable.

- It can be wise to recall some wishes that you once had, but which gladly were never satisfied.

- Five things no one can ever take from me – my experience, my memories, my education, God's love for me and my ability to love.

- We all need an adversary to wrestle with us, to strengthen and sharpen our skills.

- When things are against you, remember that aircraft take off into the wind.

- Humour is often the shortest distance between two people.

- Bread for myself is a material problem but bread for others is a spiritual one.

- Others' love for you is God's gentle helping hand on your shoulder.

- To refuse to love myself is an act of violence against my selfhood.

- A sensitive guest always makes their host feel at home.

- Some people have lost the art of conversation but not the power of speech.

- Disclosure of one's vulnerability furthers friendship and receptivity.

- Genuine listening requires a courageous open mind that is ready to change.

- When we reach out to help someone we are saying, 'This is my body being given for you'.

- An exaggerated opinion of others' happiness can lead to discontentment.

- Refusal of proffered help to a friend or from a friend can hurt.

- Experts tell us that body language carries about 60% of all communication.

- No one can give others the love I denied them.

- Keeping another person down drains your energy because of having to stay down there.

- A good friend can hold you up upside down and shake out all the nonsense.

- Real communication starts when people feel listened to, understood and accepted.

- Listening for the values, meaning and feelings of the other is true listening.

- Knowing yourself, what you believe and where you are going makes life meaningful.

- The reward of effort is not just what we gain from it but what we become by it.

- If you trim yourself to suit everybody, you will soon whittle yourself away.

- When my heart meets my neighbour's needs I am in God's will.

- Contact your friends often. Weeds grow on an unused path.

- A good friendship can be like a mountain walk – exhilarating and sometimes exhausting.

- Friendliness and cooperation do not have to include approval and affection.

- No one can make you feel inferior without your consent.

- A river without banks becomes a swamp. Some boundaries are essential.

- If you are always lonely when alone, you are keeping bad company.

- Deep listening presumes a willingness to understand and to empathize.

- The world does not owe you anything. It was here first.

- When some people cease talking, it is good not to interrupt them.

- For self and others, forward planning begins with openness and education for change.

- To accept some of our weaknesses is a requisite for happiness.

- People are more impressed by how much I care than by how much I know.

- Anger makes your mouth work faster than your mind.

- People will forget what I said but not how I made them feel.

- Every meeting with another can be changed into an encounter by sincere attention and genuine interest.

- My unwillingness to change can lead to a blatant denial of facts.

- Best leave the unchangeable alone and let fixed people be. Time is precious.

- Let no one shrink you by returning nastiness they have shown you.

- Be kind to unkind people. They need it most.

- What we push under the carpet will trip us someday.

- To be wronged is common but to keep remembering it should be rare.

- Envy of one enjoyable item or quality in another can make us miss the unpleasant experiences of that person.

- Alleviating any deprivation in the lives of others is part of the path to my salvation.

- Kind words and deeds can have a wide and a lasting effect. You never know where their influence will end.

- Some people are always me-deep in conversation.

- Happiness is an experience to be effortlessly shared.

- The greatest violence I can do another person is to despair of him or her.

- Mutual responsibility beats co-responsibility.

- If I am too big to do little things well, I am too small to do big things.

- Some people try to be other people.

- Genuine interest facilitates and deepens encounter greatly.

- Friendship is open and lasting. Passion is focused and passing.

- Keep your friendships polished by regular contacts.

- It is often good to sip out a problem with a friend.

- It takes little to fill a big heart.

- No one does anything uncharacteristic of who they are for long periods.

- Commitment demands identity. I cannot say 'forever' unless you can say 'I am'.

- Hospitality is more about time generously given than about meals shared or money passed on.

- A good conversationalist encourages others to talk.

- Many things catch your eye. Follow the things that catch your heart.

- Secrets are something told only to one person at a time.

- Carry the burden of occasional displeasure with yourself.

- In company you can communicate or miscommunicate, but you do not ever not communicate.

- You are your real self when no admirers are in sight.

- After each parting from others, do I leave light or shadow?

- Silent caring company is often more helpful than prolonged good advice.

- When you make a fool of yourself, a real friend will tell you that you have not done a permanent job.

- Much of what I am now was formed by decisions I made in the past.

- In conversation, try not make up in length for what you lack in depth.

- Lying can get you a long way but it cannot easily get you back.

- Education can begin with fruitful confusion.

- Pride, prejudice, passion or personal preference can limit the search for truth.

- Growth can come through fragility, failure, futility or falls on our journey.

- Most of our faults are more pardonable than the efforts we make to hide them.

- 75 written attempts remain of Thomas Grey's effort to produce his *Elegy in a Country Churchyard*.

- Truthful conversation encourages goodness at the heart of the human experience.

- Real love never controls and never demands perfection. It is happy with growth in freedom.

- I cannot change a painful past, but I can let it go.

- When you have failed five times, you have just found five ways that don't work.

- To be simple is to be *sine plicae* (without folds), that is, not to conceal our weaknesses.

- I must accept my limits, trust totally, hope greatly and do what I can.

- Oaks grow strong in contrary winds. Diamonds develop under pressure.

- Rational awareness is only one kind of consciousness.

- Real education takes place only in response to real need.

- Experience is a great but demanding teacher. It gives the test before the lesson.

- People who ask questions usually do not lose their way.

- Until we overcome a fixated fear of getting it wrong, we will never get it right.

- We never discover the rich oceans of life until we leave the impoverished shores of safety.

- To be without some of the things we want is indispensable to happiness.

- Regret only the experiences from which you did not learn.

- If you are not failing from time to time, you are probably working below your capacity.

- Nothing ruins the truth like stretching it.

- Wisdom is knowing when to fall short of perfection. Growth is normal.

- Apathy is becoming one of the greatest anti-growth sources of our time.

- We are made to be burdens and growth-sources to one another.

- Every great event happened when someone decided not to give up.

- Occasionally people are educated beyond their capacity to think deeply.

- Many great truths started as near-blasphemies.

- It is one thing to have truth on our side. It is another to be on the side of truth.

- People who are too embarrassed to ask questions will grow still more uninformed.

- Some people prefer the certainty of misery above the uncertainty of mystery.

- Growth towards completeness is perfection.

- The constant search for certainties can lead to anxious exhaustion.

- The difference between a weed and a flower is an opinion.

- Learn from others' mistakes. You do not have time to make them all yourself.

- After failing ten times, I have discovered ten ways that do not work.

- Co-workers may sometimes be helpful but co-walkers always are.

- Enjoy all journeys – even the detours – without fixation on the end.

- Success often means taking steps or climbing ladders rather than using the elevator.

- Minds, like parachutes, work only if they are open.

- Self-fulfilment grows from the journey towards self-transcendence.

- Change is often feared lest it disturb or dispossess.

- We grow through contemplation, compassion and creativity.

- It is always important to distinguish between motion and direction.

- To stop growing, never do anything for the first time.

- I learn little with my mouth open.

- If you do what you always did, you will always get what you got always.

- A narrow vision and a short timeframe make a closed or limited mind.

- Stagnation results from never stepping away from immediate satisfactions.

- Don't limit the challenges. Try to challenge the limits.

- An apology is often the best way to have the last word.

- Prejudice is weighing the facts with your thumb on the scales.

- Forgiveness is a decision accompanied with a mind-change or action. Feelings do not forgive.

- My conscience is all of me at my most centred free moment.

- I forgive and others forgive, but nature does not forgive.

- When you bury the hatchet, do not mark the spot.

- The light of creative altruism or the darkness of destructive selfishness always lie before us.

- Gandhi reminded us that forgiveness is an attribute of the strong.

- Repentance is not just regret about the past. It is a change of mind about the future.

- What is God for? God is for giving and forgiving.

- There is great wisdom in listening, learning and letting go.

- There is no objective vantage point from which to judge something of which we are part.

- God never forgives in the future. God has already forgiven, and we have just to acknowledge that we need to accept it.

- Muscles need gentleness in later years.

- Even as old age approaches and energy decreases, trust, thanks, prayer and patience can grow.

- Remember 'stretch or stiffen' and 'use it or lose it' after your 25th birthday.

- Love can grow forever despite my age and lessening mental or emotional energy.

- Children absorb. Adults reflect. Jesus hugged children but instructed adults.

- Scripture says that each of us is God's work of art. Art grows more beautiful with age.

- No loving parents wish their children to feel in debt to them. Nor does God.

- The memory of one's mother can make one pause before acting foolishly.

- The only trouble about retirement is that you never get a day off.

- As we mature, more things matter less, and less things matter more.

- Children may wreck a house, but they can hold a home together.

- Youth can run into difficulties. In old age difficulties tend to run into us.

- As well as giving your children flowers, teach them how to grow their own.

- Good habits developed when young make for a much smoother later life.

- Old age can be the experience of small frustrations but also of deep freedom.

- If you think you are too old to start, compare your age when the undertaking is finished with your age if you do not undertake it.

- Some people think that if they never grow up they never grow old.

- The second half of life is about losing our tethers and loosening false controls.

- A calendar shows the passing of the years; our face may show what we have done with them.

- Youthfulness is not just a time of life. It can be a state mind.

- Humans are the only creatures who welcome their children back home in adulthood. Words we speak to a child become their inner voice.

- *'Libido potestatis'* (the lust for power) is a risk for any leader.

- Authority comes from acting authentically, not from the use of power.

- Leaders need to inspire and awaken not just legislate and control.

- G. K. Chesterton warned us to beware of the blinding clarity of the madman.

- Insecure leadership says 'go'; secure leadership says 'let's go'.

- Real authority is service. It authorises growth.

- Poor leadership generates pressure and fear. Authentic leadership generates enthusiasm.

- Consult your own inner authority often and learn to trust it.

- Unthinking respect for authority could be the enemy of truth.

- When respect is absent, authority is experienced as oppression.

- If you want to get an idea across, wrap it in a pleasant person.

- Eventually every great plan needs someone to do something.

- Footprints are easier to follow than fingers.

- If you remove your title, your uniform and your admirers, what is left?

- Charm will get a speaker attention for about ten minutes. After that he or she must have something of substance to say.

- Political power combined with conventional virtue crucified Jesus.

- Keep your words soft; you may have to eat them.

- Some politicians unite their followers around enemies – scarecrow politics.

- Knowing the present experience of your audience is more important than knowing what you are going to say.

- Every decision is a little divorce.

- Fruitful knowing and doing must always involve understanding and interpretation

- The pursuit of accumulation, achievement and adulation could lead to slavery.

- He who knows how will get a job. He who knows why will get a promotion.

- Conscience and duty defend us against rigid compulsion and lingering guilt.

- The most brilliant insight could have an oversight.

- When we focus on fear, our minds become our own prisons.

- Nothing truly valuable arises from ambition or from a mere sense of duty.

- When speaking the power of pause to keep listeners' minds alert for insight must not be neglected.

- Logic can get you from A to B. Imagination can get around the alphabet.

- The captain intent on caring too much for his ship might never leave the shore.

- To fully know what one is about to do, it is important to be aware of what one might be undoing.

- Einstein said that the value of a person resides in what they give, not in what they can receive.

- Vision without action becomes a daydream. Action without vision can become a nightmare.

- Most great achievements were once considered impossible.

- In trouble, do you want to be saved by a lighthouse or by a lifeboat?

- Postage stamps stick to one thing until they get there.

- To solve a problem it can help to ask what does this problem need to survive?

- It is often difficult to choose courage and comfort at the same time.

- My silent footprints are better guides to others than my raised voice.

- In giving a talk, aim at getting attention, interest, desire and action in that order.

- My true self shows itself in the way I treat those who cannot be of any use to me.

- Unlike prejudices, convictions can be explained in a quiet voice.

- Mature people can be told uncomfortable truths about themselves.

- It is much easier to remember and repeat than to reflect and to refresh.

- What counts cannot always be counted, and what can be counted does not always count.

- Achievement comes through inspiration, aspiration, participation and perspiration.

- Facts have no hidden agenda. Face them.

- Not to decide is to decide.

- Coincidence might be God at work but wishing to remain anonymous.

- God loves me unconditionally, extravagantly and crazily by human standard.

- Calvary did not change God's mind about loving us. It revealed God's unchanging love for us.

- There was nothing – no thing – in the Holy of Holies. Only a deep personal awareness of God.

- God is neither father nor mother. God is both and God is more.

- God's plan is not an itinerary. It is attitude and loving action.

- The temple and priesthood once represented God's presence and will. Jesus is now both.

- God continually interrupts us with the needs and claims of the marginalised.

- We can meet and enjoy God without theology as we can enjoy music without a course in musicology.

- Luther said that God has written the promise of resurrection into every leaf in springtime.

- 'Earn' and 'merit' are not used in reference to God in the New Testament.

- God is not up there, out there or in there. God is wherever you are open to goodness.

- We meet God in every action on the journey to becoming human.

- Some people meet God as a demander. Some meet God as gift.

- God calls us to be welcoming witnesses of his love, not lawyers, judges or gatekeepers.

- Jesus is God's body language.

- In Jesus, we encounter full acceptance, perfect understanding with radical invitation.

- Table fellowship for Jesus was boundary breaking and communion making.

- Jesus did not say 'worship me'. He said 'follow me'.

- Jesus showed how destructive violence can be replaced by redemptive suffering.

- Jesus did not form a committee. He gave good news to a group of fishermen and told them to spread it.

- God for us we call Father. God beside us we call Son, and God within us we call Spirit.

- Our merciful God forgives not in words but by a silent embrace and celebration.

- Many people are willing to serve God, but mostly as advisors.

- No words can describe what God is.

- If God were not for freedom, divinity would be running the world.

- God will not love us more if we improve. His love invites and enables us to improve.

- God is not available to the neutral observer.

- Some of our best prayers are just a groan to God.

- Here we can see God in all things; in the next life, we will see all things in God.

- Jesus often knocks at my door to get out.

- God's felt absence is in fact God's presence.

- The existence of God cannot be proven. Only personal commitment can give us the experience of the divine.

- God created things that continue to create themselves.

- God speaks to us through creation, people, scripture, tradition and experience.

- God suffers amnesia about my confessed sins.

- My weaknesses and vulnerability are God's help to remind me of my poverty.

- Is there a God? Where does your question come from?

- Jesus said that he is not a victim. He said 'no one takes my life from me'.

- We meet God by self emptying and spiritual practices, not by abstract speculation.

- The creator of the world is never in conference when we wish to speak to him.

- God's circumference is nowhere and God's centre is everywhere.

- Idolatry arises when some image of God becomes absolutized.

- Always trust that God's address is often at the heart of what happens.

- God will not ask the name of your neighbourhood but to how many you were a neighbour.

- God's love does not depend on our growth. Divine love inspires and enables us to grow.

- The god in whom many do not believe, and in whom many believe, does not exist.

- The phrase 'Almighty God' does not appear in the Gospels or in the Epistles.

- The divine is what happens to a person on the way to becoming human.

- Sin takes us out of God's plan but never out of God's loving reach.

- God is not and not even like a superhuman being.

- The mystery of God is not something we cannot understand. It is so rich that we can never understand it enough.

- Perhaps we do not hear God's present word because we did not hear his last one.

- God will not ask the size of your home. He will ask how many people you invited in.

- If I follow Jesus, I must accept that what I do not need is not mine.

- Einstein wrote that his father's greatest praise for any new theory was that it was beautiful.

- There is no cosmetic for beauty like peace of heart.

- Like water, goodness nourishes without trying, and it is content with low places.

- Goodness has nothing to do with geography. Good people are good everywhere.

- The reign of God is thriving anywhere that there is goodness, peace and joy.

- Sometimes we give up goodness for the sake of feeling good.

- The poor have a right to bread – and to beauty.

- Arranging a bowl of flowers in the morning can permeate a day with beauty.

- A thing of beauty is often a job forever.

- Freedom consists not in doing what you choose but in having the right to do it.

- The word salvation means freedom from internal and external constriction.

- Freedom is not the capacity to review choice endlessly. It is the capacity to make choices and to pursue them.

- A friend leaves us with every freedom except the freedom not to grow.

- Do not let ambiguity, confusion or mystery ambush your journey to freedom.

- Successful democracy depends on reflection, dialogue and decision-making before it is freedom to vote for anything.

- Conversion means to keep turning back towards goodness. Most of us do it.

- We are all meant to be mothers because God and goodness continually needs to be born.

- The Talmud says that God will hold us responsible for failure to enjoy all the good things given us.

- God's final word to goodness is 'The banquet is ready.'

- Gradually replace all 'musts', 'shoulds', 'oughts' and 'have tos' with personal, moral free choices in your life.

- Sin is not so much doing evil as the misuse of what is good.

- Try to avoid a skirmish with love. Allow it to continually ambush your life.

- Love is not deeply tested until I cease expecting anything – even a response – in return.

- Shallow selfish living can bring fun, but only deep generous loving brings joy.

- Am I loved because I love, or do I only love when I am loved?

- Human interaction without love can be effective, but it is doubtfully human.

- Give your heart more exercise; stretch it by loving more.

- To love in order to be loved is a quid pro quo, a selfish existence.

- Love is a judgement, a decision and some action, not just a feeling.

- Love is not blind. It sees more deeply and more clearly, and then it sees more.

- You must be prepared to love someone before you get to know them.

- You cannot love someone you possess. The loved one must always be free.

- Our sense of sin depends not on a list but on our feeling of being loved.

- Like the light of a single candle, all the darkness of the world cannot extinguish one loving action.

- It takes more constant energy to love a person than to dominate them.

- It is not where I breathe that I live at my best. It is where I love.

- Celebration is the first and deepest response to being loved. Only then comes gratitude.

- Every decision to love must include a willingness to suffer slightly or greatly.

- Love is not something you feel about. It is something good you desire and do for others.

- We are hominized by being loved in the womb and humanized by loving one another.

- Loving criticism is designed to help, not to humiliate.

- Opponents are not always enemies. We all need loving reviewers.

- Loving is always a self-enlarging experience.

- Don't cry for too long when something beautiful ends or a dear friend dies. Rejoice and be grateful that the beautiful happened.

- Do not fear death. Rather fear having lived without ever having loved.

- Life never rewards us for things we intended to do.

- Life's deep question – what am I doing for others?

- A question deep in all of us is will someone cry when I die?

- Life is a slow-release miracle.

- Life is ideally a journey away from all within that shackles us.

- Life can be understood backwards, but it must be lived forward.

- Happy people are usually grateful, but more deeply, grateful people are always happy.

- The link between life and happiness is service.

- Living realistically is like licking honey off thorns.

- Ideally, life is defenceless dedication to loving.

- Life is not accompanied by inescapable certitudes but by visions, risks and passion.

- Accepting and relishing the insecurities of life is part of life's security.

- My attitude influences my life more than any circumstances.

- Life is not a dress rehearsal.

- Dream as if you will live forever. Act as if you will die tomorrow.

- Deaths from the crash of 300 jumbo jets would not exceed the deaths from hunger each day.

- Even perfect friendship carries the future pain of parting by death.

- Thoughts that are foolish in the light of death are foolish in themselves.

- Some people try to live by lifeless clichés and meaningless jargon.

- Partings, great and small, temporary and permanent are a part of every life.

- Life is what is happening while you are worring.

- When we live more deeply within, we live more simply without.

- Better to struggle with the devil at the heart of humanity than to enjoy the angels at the edge of life.

- Do not live your life as if you had another in the bank.

- Life is deeds not just words, thoughts not just breaths, and never just dates on a calendar.

- If your mind is near the gutter, your life could go down the drain.

- Without purpose, direction and decision, life is a rocking horse – moving but going nowhere.

- Evolution is a constant revelation of divine creativity in the cosmos.

- The cosmos is no more an accident than an explosion in a printing factory could create the Oxford dictionary.

- Everything in the cosmos was perfectly prepared and ready for our coming.

- There are still endless questions that neither science, scripture nor Church can answer.

- Each of us is part of the earth's self-consciousness.

- Aiming at constant enjoyment leads to a life of continual neurosis.

- My life is no flickering candle giving light to a few. It is a fire that can warm numberless others even after I die.

- A reflected life is a continual consciousness of contingency.

- Life becomes more purposeful when it is prayer-conditioned.

- Growing in the art of dispossession prepares us for the final letting go of death.

- Life is 10% how you make it but 90% how you take it.

- Life is not the number of breaths you take but the number of times it takes your breath away.

- Fear not that your life will come to an end. Rather fear that it never has a real beginning.

- Most of life is not against us. Take off your skepticles.

- A woodpecker gets through by using his head.

- Principles do not dispense with probing into all of life's problems.

- A problem blocks my path. A mystery envelops me.

- A mosquito can make you like flies better.

- Don't follow your dreams. Chase them.

- All of art and most of good conversation is knowing when to stop.

- Beware of people who seek the intimacy of an octopus.

- Common sense is genius dressed in its working clothes.

- The punishment for desire is desire itself.

- If you think you can or think you can't, you are usually right.

- History is littered with experts who got it wrong.

- Hope can be a dark tunnel experience.

- There is need for caution where angels tread delicately.

- There is no fun in medicine but fun is good medicine.

- Shape is something you stay within if you stay without.

- The beginning of wisdom is to have a good look at the obvious.

- Being beside yourself could make a very unattractive couple.

- How much do very rich people usually leave? All of it.

- The slow mouse got the cheese.

- Anxiety can sometimes be a substitute for action.

- Wondering keeps your wits warm and your mind alert.

- Happy people can enjoy the scenery even when lost on a detour.

- Naivete and enthusiasm are a lethal cocktail.

- Don't push your luck. Sometimes it is better to move the ladder.

- Some days you are the pigeon. Some days you are the statue.

www.messenger.ie